Poetry From The Heart
(The Truth Of The Matter)
Volume 1

Published by
Ofafu
7552 Brentwood Stair Rd.
Fort Worth, TX 76112
4049 Piedmont Drive
New Orleans, LA 70122
Cover Photo © 2015 Nnamdi Jude Odelugo

Table of Contents

Table of Contents continued

Time

How quickly the days do come and go,
Yesterday being never more.

Tomorrows are what we all hope for,
Though soon becoming the days that were.

Time passes on but never ends,
It only tells us where it's been.

It does not drag, nor does it stop,
It will not skip, it will not hop.

This fleeting gift that's so controlled,
This gift of time we cannot hold.

May 21, 1990

The Woman Inside

We go through life wanting to be held,
Our bodies cry out but who can tell?
We have a natural tendency for affection and love,
Oh how nice it is to be squeezed and hugged.

Sometimes we pretend to be strong and brave,
When deep down inside we're oh so scared.
Much too often we make decisions and plans,
Needing so desperately, loving helping hands.

The woman inside is often thought to be,
One of complexity, as sturdy as a tree.
But the woman we are is not hard to figure out,
A little love and kindness will tell you what we're about.

We take delight in pleasing those we love,
Reciprocation need be only a kiss and a hug.

We are quick to make sacrifices for those of our own,
Especially toward the children even when they are born.
They come into the world so dependent on us,
Often times their entrance causes great fuss.

No matter how tired and spent we are,
We hold them close out of concern, out of love.
As they go through life continuing to grow,
There comes a time when we hardly know them anymore.

Sometimes we reflect back to when they were born,
And we ask ourselves what could have gone wrong.

The Woman Inside
continued

To the woman inside it's hard to let go,
Of the ones she love and nurtured so.
But facing realities she puts on a front,
Falling in line with others through sighs and grunts.

I guess the woman inside will always be,
To many of the unconcerned a mystery.
Sometimes we can't help but sit and cry,
Don't ask us why, it's just the woman inside.

February 17, 1990

Me and My Pearls

As I sat quietly watching the rain,
My mind is drifting and I feel no pain.
It is truly times like this,
That should be shared with the tenderest kiss.

Ever since I was a little girl,
I've always made the rain drops my pearls.
As the rain would fall upon my window pane,
I would drift away into lovely wonderlands.

No one could ever see,
Just what the rain drops meant to me.
The value of my pearls have been as such,
That poverty is none, but riches are much.

I've been to places where many could not afford,
I've walked through the forest with someone whom I've adored.

I've eaten the best foods and drank the choicest wines,
I've been taken to places where only queens would dine.

I can only hope as time goes by,
That nothing comes between my pearls and I.

My first poem

What Ought To Be

Don't give me my birds in a cage,
For this purpose they were not made.

You clip their wings and they're no longer free,
Oh how selfish we humans can be.

Do observe them from afar,
Creatures of flight is what they are.

Their beauty abounds everywhere,
To contain such beauty is not very fair.

A variety of colors is breath taking to behold,
The number runs high for these little souls.

Instinctively they keep their distance from us,
In human beings they do not trust.

I contemplate the day when this will change,
I look forward to the birds eating from my hands.

Assuredly I put faith in the prophecies,
They tell us how things ought to be.

In Days to Come

They summoned the folks to all come down, to see if their love ones could be found. Their strides were slow their faces wore a frown, as they began to take a slow look around.

In my minds own eyes I try to see, the day when tragedies will no longer be. The fear of intruders will be no more, only the trusted will grace one's door.

The sleepless nights, the troubled days, forever will be taken out one's way. No longer will money be the thing in which people put their sole trust in. Gone will be the ones in public eyes, the ones always saying, "Come on come buy."

The homeless ones will have found their place, not even one being considered a case. No more will hospitals be in need, sickness and death will be gone indeed.

With eagerness of heart I contemplate the day, when the innocent ones are no longer prey. No longer will anyone need an alarm, there's no one there to do them harm. However good only the hopes of some to soon be realized in days to come.

August 1, 1990

The Final Say

What a sight a sight to behold,
People working together both young and old.
They're all doing whatever they can,
With heartfelt appreciation just to lend a hand.
Some are working with skills they've earned,
Others are there with eagerness to learn.
They all come together to fill a certain need,
To build a place of worship where people can feed.
To feed on God's word is beyond compare,
So out of brotherly love they all have a share.
This performance is seen throughout the earth,
Indicating to the world that some are alert.
They apply God's word in their daily lives,
So faithfully they know he could never lie.
As the world observes this marvelous work,
Some are impressed but others provoked.
But this building work will continue to grow,
Until God himself says no more.

Mama Dee Bauman
Saturday, September 28, 2013

Once Upon A Time

Once upon a time my grandmother would say,
Things were so different in my day.
I remember with sheer delight,
The good times we had both day and night.

Playing in the rain was a longed for treat,
Sitting by the fireplace just warming our feet.

Mama in the kitchen baking gingerbread,
While visions of childhood danced in our heads.

We had no worry about this or that,
We saw life as it was that's a fact.
There wasn't any TV. to worry about,
Mama got her news from the market shop.

Sundays were our very special day,
With lots of good food to eat but not much play.
We managed somehow to stay clean all day,
Which wasn't easy since we loved to play.

Relatives would visit from everywhere,
Sometimes we hardly knew they were there.
We were so involved in our own little games,
To us grown up talk wasn't the same.

They never had to run us out of sight,
We knew just when to take a hike.
When things settled down and all was quiet,
We got ready for bed oh so tired.

Life was good to us back then,
Once upon a time, God knows when.

June 24, 1989

The Do Drop Inn

It has been said about this house many a times,
Unlocked doors is what you'll find.
Over the years it's been that way,
Someone is there on any given day.

The children are the ones that frequent there,
Hospitality there is never rare.
It's just an ordinary looking house you see,
But it's a place where many like to be.

It's not uncommon to receive a call,
From someone in need and that's not all.
Many of the calls come from the schools,
Send someone to get me, considered the rule.

I view this house as one of a kind,
No fussing, no cussing, no pollution you'll find,
The aroma of food will greet you there,
The occupants there are those who care.

The meager furniture within is holding its own,
Not of great importance in making this house a home.
Although some might be critical of such,
But in the attitude of others I worry not much.

Child abuse there unheard of for sure,
Should one attempt this feat, they're quickly shown the door.

But all and all this house pleases not everyone,
Especially those not fearing God and his Son.
Talking against our God we won't tolerate,
This is something we really do hate.

This house is all about making friends,
Where the welcome mat says the Do Drop In.

March 15, 1990

12

Life is Hard

Life is hard no one can doubt, especially when love ones move about.
Drifting here and drifting there so determined not to share.

Life is hard when things go wrong, even the birds seems to loose their song.

Standing on a hilltop, one can see quite far, but down on the ground you can
hardly see a star. But just to know that they exist, lets us know that God
hasn't missed. His desire was for man to have what was good, but some how
they never quite understood. They push ahead all on their own, ignoring
God's words found in the Psalms.

Life is hard beyond a shadow of a doubt, to know this fact shouldn't make
us pout. It should move us to action without delay, showing love for one
another in our own special way. Not isolating ones self to our own demise,
but sticking close to whatever makes us wise.

Life is hard in these critical times, but loving God's Laws gives us peace of
mind. Being in his service there's so much to do, with many blessings ahead
for me and you.
Yes life is hard some might say, but life is the gift that God gives so don't
throw it away.

June 21, 1989

What About Love?

Just what is love all about?
That makes some quiet, while it makes others shout.

It makes some weep, and moan for days,
It causes many to change their ways.

Love is so wonderful yet so sad,
One day you're happy the next day so mad.

Love is something so very, very unique,
But most of the time so very hard to keep.

Whenever I think of love and the way it was,
Right away my heart begins to buzz.

I recall some days unlike the rest,
I remember how love made me feel my best.

Love is quite confusing to most,
But love is something in which to boast.

Not all will experience the privilege of such,
And to all such ones the lost is much.

When love falls on responsible hearts,
It creates a bond never to part.
It causes concerned ones to do their best,
Especially when their love is put to the test.

So just like the days that turns into nights,
Love is never wrong, but always right.

March 22, 1990

Mirroring

Why do you ask me how I feel?
Then you're left without words when I tell
you what's real.

Could it be just a formality?
That you pretend to be concerned about me.

And why do I feel the need to lie,
Just what am I trying to hide?

I act as if I am ashamed of me,
Ashamed to be dependent, in need.

Sometimes I am as depressed as one can be,
I ask the infamous question why me?
I look around and I think I see,
Everyone else doing better than me.

But in my heart I can clearly see,
That this is not reality.
It is so refreshing when certain ones come along,
Or simply to call me on the phone.

They seem to know just what it is,
And they have no advice to give.
The feelings pour out back and forth,
Without the aid of written notes.

And what do you know before too long,
You come to know, you're not alone.
We mirror, we talk, we empathize,
We listen, we share, we tell no lies.

Written in behalf of my Friend and Spiritual Sister,
Ollie Givens

October 22, 1997

Love Lives On

We try to prepare the best that we could,
Doing what we thought we should.
But how does one prepare for something like this,
Toward someone who'll be dearly missed.

How do we pick up the pieces and carry on,
After our loved one is gone?

We think about the days we shared with them,
We think about the undying love of a friend.
The love of a friend goes on and on,
Carrying us through even after they're gone.

Although in their lives we no longer may have a part,
But they will always have a place in our hearts.
Our God knows who we are even before we are born,
He gives us strength beyond our own.

He remembers the tears that one has shed,
And all the sacrifices that they had made.

In God's undying memory may they now rest on,
Awaiting for the sound of the trumpet's horn because love lives on.

(Gone but not forgotten Praise Jah, the God of all comfort)

To Be a Parent

We raise our children the best we can,
Needing so desperately loving helping hands.
God's word is what we need the most,
From there we will learn just how to cope.

Sometimes we pretend to be strong and brave,
When deep down inside we're oh so scared.
Our children are a possession we should all hold dear,
But sometimes it's so hard just to keep them near.

Our sacrifices and our love sometimes is not enough,
It tends to make life kind of tough.
But we hang in there trying to do our best,
Our children are entitled to nothing less.

We can only hope and pray,
That things would get better someday.
Keeping in mind a saying so true,
It's not so much what happens in life, but what we do.

A Friend in Need

Once in a lifetime someone like you comes along,
It almost sounds like the words of a song.
Songs should be written about someone like yourself,
Someone who knows the meaning of help.

Unreservedly you stepped right in,
No one could hope for a better friend
You consistently never tire out,
You are a stickler for making things right.

We all feel blessed because of you,
May Jehovah continue to bless what you do.
May he strengthen you when things get out of hand,
May he strengthen us to reciprocate in your behalf the same.

I feel that we are in a win win situation,
Doing what you do out of sincere compassion.
Your personality speaks tons about who you are,
As you go through life keep your sense of humor.
A household word your name has become,
The same in our home, we will always say to you Steve Bowman welcome.

August 7, 2013

Gone But Not Forgotten

Years ago when I was oh so young,
Those were truly the days of fun.
Running around in our bare feet,
Having no fear at all of playing on the street.

In those days our doors were never locked,
No keys were used to get in or out.
Barred up windows and doors never came to mind,
We really thought that life was fine.

A little something extra was expected by all,
Lagniappe is what it was called.
That quality of life existed back then,
Most of our neighbors acted like kin.

It didn't take much to satisfy us,
We expected whatever we got without any fuss.
But however good it saddens me some,
I now realize that more could have been done.

In those days many were shunned,
No one told us we are all God's unique creation.
They failed to show us just how to be proud,
The examples they set didn't teach us how.

Many times they made us lie for them,
Go tell the bill collectors I'm not in.
They didn't tell me I was worth waiting for,
When the time arrived, no was not my answer.

My indiscretion I tried to hide,
As my precious baby grew inside.
After a while no one was fooled,
As innocence was born into a world so cruel.

Gone But Not Forgotten
continued

So much to be learned, so much to do,
Mistakes were anything but few.

As I ponder those days of long ago,
I bid them farewell, forever more.

Things That Make Me Glad

Whenever my family get together and I hear the noise,
It's the kind of noise that brings me joy.
They mainly talk about things of the past.
For some reason or another, this makes them laugh.

To just see how they relate with one another,
Should bring pleasure to any loving mother.
IT makes me glad to know they
Are being cared for,
Caring for each other out of love.
IT makes me glad just knowing
Where my children are,
Even though they are not children anymore.
I don't worry about them driving drunk,
To even think about doing that I don't.
The grandchildren follow in the pattern
Of their parents,
They too are blessed with common sense.
These are some of the things that me glad,
But for those who don't have what I have,
It makes me sad.

December 5, 2012

Imperfect As We Are

Imperfect as we are there still exist this thing called love.
Sometimes we forget just how important it is,
Then we act as if we have nothing to give.
We may wonder about this or that,
Causing us in an unfavorably way to act.
Imperfect as we are, we can rise above this lack of love.
If we let it be a permanent thing,
The hearts of others we can hope to win.
Such love is motivated by what we do today,
Fifteen years of togetherness what more can one say.
We can say what a fine example you've made,
You have avoided any defilement of your sacred bed.
You make me proud just to know you are mine,
Our relationship is one of a kind.
Imperfect as we are, we are governed by the love from above,
May the rest of your years turn out to be,
A fine example for others to see.
May all of your endeavors prove to be wise,
Being looked on favorably in Jehovah's eyes.
As I penned down these words I'm thinking again,
Brian you've turned out to be a fine young man.
Victoria what can I say about you,
that you are the same no matter what life brings you.
So hang in there my children,
Love what God loves and hate what He hates.
Then you will never go wrong together as mates.

Find Your Own Aha Moment in Life

Everyone should have their aha moment in life,
It's the thing that lets you know what's right.
It's that deep feeling inside your gut,
Falling for one's looks is just not enough.
You need to know if he or she is the right one,
Because falling for the wrong one is no fun.
My aha moment came one day out of the blue,
My husband told me about the things he used to do.
He said before he knew me, he feared no one,
But on one particular day he faced a guy with a gun.
And for the first time in his life,
He said he feared for his life,
The look on his face let me know, he was the one I loved for sure.
After that particular day,
Other aha moments came my way.
Standing by my stove one day just thinking about him coming home,
Just thinking about him I felt no longer alone.
Aha moments can come in many ways,
A certain look across the room, something special that was said.
Those getting married should look for their aha moment,
It may be hard to find so take your time.
Aha moments may be hard to find,
But they are important as can be,
Ask the woman inside, ask me.

June 16, 2015

Let's Help Our Brain

Many women work out of necessity,
That was the case when it came to me.
Many nights of traveling on the bus from work to home,
There were times my life was in ways of harm.

One night in particular I'll never forget,
No one on the street walked faster than me had I ever met.
But this night things changed,
I was being out walked by tall young man.

At first I didn't realize what he was up to,
I had to figure out what to do.
My mind was racing like never before,
Should I knock on someone's door, or should I just continue to go?

When I crossed over he crossed over too,
At this time I didn't know exactly what to do.
At the same time he made his move grabbing me with both hands,
I couldn't believe I was being attacked by this man.,
With no time to waste I pushed him out of my face.
Pretending to have something in my purse but he called my bluff.

In an instant I caught sight of someone I knew,
At this time the man took flight and flew.
It's amazing what the brain goes through at times like this,
Clear thinking turns out to be a miss.
Perhaps the only way to help one's brain,
Is to think about what we would do beforehand.

Living Next Door To Your House

When I moved next door to your house,
My uncertainties were many, and so were my doubts.

But as the days turned into months,
My anxieties grew less, we really had fun.

And as the months passed into years,
Your remarkable conduct stilled my fears.

Living next door to someone like you,
Have proved to be a very smart move.

I delight in seeing my grandchildren grow,
And to be a part of their lives I hope forever more.

I know that I am blessed to have so much,
When others have much less.
I hope whatever our destinies turn out to be,
That you've also enjoyed living next door to me.

They Speak Without Words

Speak out oh you silent lights,
Tell about God's glory both day and night.
He gives you to us so abundantly,
No other place would I want to be.

At the close of each day I know without a doubt,
That somewhere over this earth your faces shines out.

Although you are the lesser one,
Your purpose, your glory is never done.
You fulfill your duties so orderly,
You always manage to impress little me.

Your true companion the greater one,
Meets our needs when night is done.
Even though you are separate in form,
I thank Jehovah God for the day you were born.

I thank Him for letting you shine upon me,
Without your presence where would any of us be.
So keep on speaking about the glory of our God,
Speaking out in silence from so very high above.

October 8, 1989

Silent Cries

Hush little babies don't you cry,
It's not your fault you have to die.

Blame it on your mommies, blame it on your dads',
Blame it on those who've made you a fad.

But I just want to let you know,
There's coming a time when this will be no more.

No more will cries like yours be heard,
On that you have God's own written word.

So hush now babies, close your eyes,
Because our God has heard your silent cries.

February 4, 1990

Menopause

A female in heat is what we are,
And this has nothing to do with love.
We wake up in the morning sweating from head to toe,
Thinking to ourselves I just can't take it anymore.
We try our best to keep afloat, trying hard just to cope.
Little things tend to get next to us,
Making it hard for us not to fuss.
Our mate gets the brunt of our revolt,
But shouldn't they know it's not our fault.
Facial make-up is not our friend,
Sweat and powder do not blend.
Being a female we get the raw end of the deal,
Eve in the garden our faith she did seal.
So what can be said about the state we are in,
Maybe just to wish that menopause was for men.

December 5, 2012

Why Do People Value Worthless Things

Why do people value worthless things?
It's almost like asking why do birds sing.
Some worthless things come with a price,
Like the toss of a coin, or the roll of the dice.

Most worthless things are poorly made,
Lasting only briefly, so quickly they fade.
Those giving in to such pursuits,
The numbers run high just check their roots.

They follow a definite pattern it seems,
Placing insurmountable value on getting the green.
Worthless things are so easy to obtain,
The world thinks everyone feels the same.

The saying goes that the majority rules,
Perhaps that's why there's so many fools.
So quickly they rush into harms way,
Doing their own thing most would say.

They so much want to be like the rest,
Creating for themselves one big mess.
Worthless things come with a disguise,
But not cleaver enough to fool the wise.

Why Do People Value Worthless Things
continued

Those without insight are easily mislead,
Because worthless things comes as a fad.
Many are the ones falling in line,
A lack of appreciation is what you'll find.

In pursuit of such things many have gone astray,
Being caught up in the crowd on that broad and spacious way.

One fact remains, and that's for sure,
You can't take it to the bank
As the saying goes.
In answer to the question posed at the start,
Why do people value worthless things?
Because they're just not smart.

March 16, 1990

Montezuma's Revenge

Beads of sweats roll down my face,
A hurry, a hurry, with no time to waste.

A tumultuous war is brewing inside,
My anxieties, my feelings, I cannot hide.

No time to stop, no time to think,
But what oh what did I eat or drink.

What did I do to stir up such a rage,
A revengeful rage that respects no age.

I am determined to put up a pretty good fight,
I just hope it doesn't last throughout the night.

Although I've had this battle before,
Still it caught me unprepared for sure.

I guess in the future my defense should be,
To be very very careful to what I put inside of me.

April 1, 1992

Do Give Me My Roses In Life

Such a beautiful array of flowers I see,
Gods' creations impresses me.
As I gaze upon the stillness of her face,
I wonder if these flowers are just a waste.

I wonder how many she received in life,
Perhaps quite a few, she was such a good wife.
The soft music that's playing befits her style,
If she was here with us her face would wear a smile.

As I look at the faces of the bereaved,
They all seem to be greatly grieved.
This is a sobering time indeed,
It brings to mind one's own time to leave.

Making us think about our own lot in life,
It's only in living can we make things right.
Only in living can we feel the sun,
Praising our god for all he has done.

Only in living can we love one another,
Only in living can we help our brother.
It's only in living can we do our best,
Having no earthly control over the rest.

It's only for the living at a time like this,
That will feel the sadness that will feel the miss.
So as we live, do let us live,
Because only in living can we hope to give.

May 29, 1993

No Time to Waste

What merits does complexity hold?
Standing there trying to look so bold.

It gives off the pretense of trying to be,
The true evaluation for one to see.

It sits there saying "It is I only I,
The thing in which to be guided by.

Think not that truth holds the clue,
It's just too simple, it will not do".

But in spite of the acclaim it holds by some,
Not cleaver enough to fool everyone.

Complexity, the force that makes one think,
There just has to be a hidden missing link.

To put complexity in its place,
Is to say my time I will not waste.

August 4, 1990

Well Done

April 10 Nisan Fourteen,
The skies above were looking so mean.
The blackest of clouds appeared so fast,
I wondered just how long they would last.

As we prepared to celebrate the Lord's evening meal,
For true Christians around the world, an event so real.
We look forward to this day once every year,
Especially as the end draws so near.

We reflect on the Memorial of Christ death,
To be celebrated right after the sun sets.
The celebration itself is a sobering affair,
We think about our sins that Jesus did bear.

Just to be counted among that great crowd,
Makes one feel oh so proud.
This year 1990 is just like the rest,
Most of those attending endeavors to look their best.
It is truly a day deserving of such,
The God we serve deserves so much.

He sent his son to die for us,
This God of love, a God so just.
We concentrate on family members we love so dear,
Hoping that they would give a receptive ear.

Letting God's truth reach their hearts,
Helping them see, our battle is being fought.
By Jesus our exemplar and our lead,
Following him so closely paying special heed.

The blood of Jesus made it possible for us all,
To take advantage of his message beckoning his call.

As we sing the "Bread From Heaven" so clear,
A song that we all hold dear.

34

Well Done
continued

In unison this song is sung,
Praising God for sending his son.

Prayers are said over the bread and wine,
The sacrifices of Jesus to be one of a kind.
The celebration itself passes by fast,
But the significance of such will always last.
It will last until Jehovah and his Son,
Looks down on us and say well done.

April 21, 1990

The Ways of a Man

The ways of a man, who can understand?
One thing is clear, so many act the same.
I have often wondered just what it is,
That makes it so hard for some men to give.

So often a man cannot decide,
The one who'll forever stay by his side.
Most of the time she's the one,
Who'll be right there when the day is done.

Because of herself, she's misunderstood,
A likely observation when one is good.
She's thought of as being satisfied with less,
Her man does not care that she craves the best.

She goes through life unappreciated for sure,
By the very ones she loves the more.
On the other side of the matter there seems to be,
The man being all that he can be.
Especially toward the ones forever in want,
His wallet is what she consistently haunt.

No matter if he works until he drops,
Concern, her not if she wants to shop.
The man will always prove to be,
Somewhat of a mystery.
But when all that is said and done,
There remains to be only one.
No matter what she'll stay the same,
Because she well knows the ways of a man.

May 8, 1990

Never Ending

As the sun slowly rises in the east,
I am clinging to this moment of peace.
Before too long as the day progress,
There won't be much time for rest.

So much depends on the mother's hand,
Taking care of the children, also the man.
A mother's role is never through,
Deeply involved in what others do.

She gives of herself both night and day,
Some will have it no other way.
On the abilities of her so many depends,
Making her role one that never ends.

May 1990

To Spoil the Child

So many times I've heard it said,
Put that child on the bed.
Ignore their cries, don't give in,
In fear of certainly spoiling them.

But just when does one spoil a child?
Could it be after holding them for a while?
Do we really spoil by fulfilling a need?
And who can really ignore a plead?

Coming from someone who cannot talk,
They cannot crawl, or even walk.
Should anyone think that they know so much?
In the opinion of themselves they put their trust.

Let's think about where that child has been,
So closely confined from within.
A bond that one cannot deny,
To ignore this fact is to close one eyes.

If only we would grasp the realities of life,
Putting all things in its proper light.
We would not fail a crucial test,
At a time when we should do our best.

To Spoil the Child
continued

I perceive that when we spoil a child,
Is after they've been here quite a while.
When we as patents fail to recognize,
What's the most important in their lives.

When we fail to remember the do's and don'ts,
Especially concerning the things they want.
When we fail to make our yes mean yes, and our no mean no,
When you tell them to come, most times they'll go.

Sometimes we fail to see the light,
Unable to see what's wrong from right.
We might be pronged to reason on such,
To overload our children since we didn't have much.

When we cater to their wants and not their needs,
They do become very spoiled indeed.

July 17, 1990

The Kind of Friend I Would Like to Have

Someone who adds a lot of joy to living,
Someone who doesn't mind giving.
A true companion that is loving all the time,
And when it comes to being loyal they would never mind.

When things don't go well and I feel depressed,
A good friend would make me feel my best.

Someone to warn me of danger and help me escape it,
Someone whom I could share my thoughts with.

I would like to have a friend like David had in Jonathan,
Who loved David like a son.

But when all that's said and done,
To have a good friend, I must be one.

Written for Tianay by DelRoBa

Only Human

We come into existence all naked and bare,
Not a worry the world, not even a care.

Our lives are not that of our own,
In total dependency we are born.

We are pronged to need love from those who care,
Reciprocation would be quite fair.

We try to adjust to this very strange scene,
Equipped with this body called a human being.

Sometimes no matter how hard we try,
We just can't help but wail and cry.
The problems we may at first create,
Will soon pass over, please have a little faith.

If ever you think about putting us out of sight,
Please abandon that thought, put up a hard fight.

Whenever we tend to get next to you,
Do keep in mind, we're only human too.

February 5, 1990

In Him We Do Boast

What can be said about living in critical times,
It covers a large area eventually you will find.
Even though war remains a threat,
So many other things caused one to fret.

Just to pick a few from the top of my head,
I'll start with food shortage, the absence of bread.
We see millions now dying from a definite lack of,
Because of greediness of others and a stark absence of love.

The children are the ones who suffer the most,
Coming into a world with Satan as its host.

Looking at the other side of the coin,
Riches are what many do yearn.
We cannot minimize the damage it's caused to some,
The realization of such, leaves me numb.

I must not forget about violence and crime,
Today a person's life isn't worth a dime.
One would think with that thought in mind,
To treat each other better, trying hard to be kind.

But according to the Bible that won't be so,
Sinful inclinations rises to the foe.
But faithful ones can rest assure,
That better days are coming forever more.

In Him We Do Boast
continued

Forever more will there no more be,
Conditions that hurt you and me.
No more will a hungry child be found,
With an abundance of food for everyone around.

When that day comes, critical times will be gone,
And according to the Bible that won't be too long,
So hang in there all you ones of faith,
Continue to love what God loves, and hate what he hates.

And in the midst of these times, critical at the most,
Continue to trust in God, in Him we do boast.

Words of Broadness

The word appreciation comes to mind,
A possession of few so sad to find.
Especially among our children it's found to be true,
Their behavioral display proves that they do.

Sometimes when asked to form a simple task,
Their faces turn into a different mask.
Spontaneous reaction is grounded in their seed,
In the case when there's something they claim to need.

To be appreciative and show that they care,
On their own most would not dare.
I can't help but wonder and ponder over such,
Since it involves those we love so much.

Our children a possession we love so dear,
In Jehovah God we hope they would learn to fear.
By applying God's word can they ever overcome,
The desires of the flesh so prevalent with some.

This word appreciation covers a lot of ground,
So sad it's not more readily found.

February 21, 1990

And They Talk About Peace

All around this universe so grand,
Lies many a problems that perplexes man.
But to admit this fact most would not dare,
They want the world to think they're going somewhere.

But one does not have to look too far,
To see that we remain under the threat of war.
Warfare and food shortages are all around,
With diseases and pestilences close behind.

As we watch the news from day to day,
Peace is what they're trying to say.
Just how can they sell this idea to most,
Such persuasions, such influences, you wonder from what source.
We can learn about this source with no stones unturned,
Reading God's word, there's so much to learn.

When man talk of peace we won't be mislead,
Jesus is our Prince of Peace our leader, our head.
We are taught to put our trust in no other source,
Jehovah and his Son the ones in which to boast.

The conditions of this world so sad indeed,
But soon now God will fill our needs.
By applying Godly wisdom in our daily lives,
Makes us without a doubt very wise.

And They Talk About Peace
continued

Wise for salvation in our creator's eyes,
Standing firm in the midst of so many lies.

So when man talks about peace in a peaceful world,
We immediately reflect back to men of old.
God's prophets tell us many years ago,
That these conditions we now face would be just so.

They tell us how man "would grow faint out of fear,"
Fear because the end is so very very near.
The end of this system is imminent indeed,
But God promises to bless Abraham's seed.

The hope of all mankind lies in God's word,
To think that he would lie, is something so absurd.
God's promise is to the obedient ones,
A Kingdom hope in the hands of his Son.

So when man talk about achieving this peace for all,
We can almost hear the roar of their fall.
To bring about peace is not in the power of man,
Only Jehovah God and his son Jesus Christ can.

Keep On Keeping On

When you keep on doing the things that are right,
Though some days are dark there's still much light.

When you keep on walking in the name of our God,
Directing all prayers through our most precious Lord,

When it seems like life has become humdrum,
Just think about the pitiful plight of some.

You know that life is give and take,
Oh how nice it is to be given a break.

When we keep in mind what's expected of us,
And we seek out those that we can trust.

When we keep our eyes fixed on the prize,
It shows that we are truly wise.
So when it seems that you're in one big rut,
Just keep on keeping on no matter what.

July 30, 1989

In This Stream of Time

When I see you walking down the street,
My heart skips a frightful beat.

Especially when there's more than one of you,
I am fearful at what you might do.

A sad, sad reality we now must face,
A reality that befalls every single race.

The innocent ones are suffering the most,
The wicked have Satan as their host.

The Bible book of Psalms helps us all to see,
That very soon now the wicked ones will cease to be.

The Woes of a Mother

The woes of a mother run very deep,
The care of her family she tries hard to keep.
But not matter how hard she tries,
Someone's not satisfied someone will cry.

She's tugged at from every end,
Everyone's need she's supposed to mend.
Nothing short of genius is expected of her,
She exists sometimes in the absence of love.

She seeks advice from here and there,
Just trying to figure what's fair.
She's misunderstood by her boys,
When they run to play in the street with their ball,
She would like to protect them from any hurt at all.

When her sons take brides of their own,
In their lives she feels she doesn't belong.
I guess it all has to do with letting go,
The things we mothers are most noted for.

I applaud the man, who stays a man,
He never forgets from once he came.
A mother's love is set for life,
But often times she feels stripped of her life.
She has a right to expect thoughtfulness and care,
From the ones she brought into the world all naked and bare.

She has a right to be thought of in a loving way,
Before the coming of her dying day.
From the rib of a man the woman came,
From the belly of the woman came the man.
I look forward to the day when I will hear no more,
Of any mother would have to suffer any more woes.

The Children of Today

What can be said about the children of today,
So many would like to have their own way.
Most are rebellious unable to teach,
Babies being strolled on a leash.

Their hearing seems to be the most impaired,
Requesting their attention, you only get a stare.
The children of today unthankful at the most,
Appreciation from them comes not without force.

We're not altogether blameless of such,
As parents we tend to give too much.
Sometimes we fail to deal with their needs,
Overlooking those many unfinished deeds.

Of course they're born at a critical time,
Reason number one for such confused minds.
I try to view them in the proper light,
Trying hard to understand their unpredictable plight.

Their schooling leaves much to be desired,
Many fall short no matter how hard they try.
The system deals in favoritism and that's not all,
They cater to the ones running with the ball.

We wish that our children could mend their ways,
But it's oh so hard in these last critical days.

The Children of Today

Children today are in need of help,
Coming from a source not of themselves.
They must look to God for He is good,
With Him they are never misunderstood.

Deep into their hearts is what He observes,
Drawing them to Him by means of His word.
But thanks to Jah there's coming a time,
When the children of today will be just fine.

March 21, 1990

Family
By Michelle Lee Ross

Oh times like these we sit and laugh
And talk about yesterday
With long lost friends and distant family
I don't know what I'd do if I wasn't a part of it
As I sit in the corner...I'm holding back the tears
All the while taking it all in...I shall hold this memory dear
For if it never happens again
At least I can say it happened
In the end that's all we need
As we leave and go to our perspective homes
Now Though I'm in this house full of people...I still feel so alone
I guess that's just the way life is
People come and go...as they wish
Even though at times it's hard to say goodbye
Sometimes even the strongest began to have tears well up in their eyes
And they began to cry
Saying see you later alligator
Hoping not to long afterward we will be reunited again
But until then at least we have all the memories
And I will hold them dear to me for an eternity

Working With Undesirables
By Nnamdi Jude Odelugo

O my goodness, it's time to start my day,
I have to go to my job where I feel a certain way.
Scanning and counting is all that we're supposed to do,
But on some of these assignments we turn into maids and butlers too.

Some of these jobs can be so draining,
When you're working with people with no home training.
Sometimes the job can make you feel that you're going to choke,
And it doesn't help when majority of these people smoke.

These are the days that you won't get back,
I really wish that some of my co-workers would stay on track.
They're talking and giggling, finding the littlest stupid thing funny,
All I want to do is count and make my money.

As I'm here doing my job, I'm thinking: "It's hard to believe that these people were hired"?
Oh how I wish that all of them would of been fired.
From the lazy to the rude, they all need to go,
Especially the socialites who always make the day seem slow.

There's honest working people working their minds and bodies to the bone,
They also wish that these undesirables would leave them would them alone.
Smoking and complaining seems to be their lot in life,
They don't even realize that they cause their own strife.

On this job, you can take some of the lessons you learn to heart,
O my goodness, I wish these undesirables would do their part.
I wish these undesirables would show that they're all in,
Instead they're all acting like farts in the wind.
All in all what can I say,
Except to wish for a better day.

May 31, 2016

Today Is The Day
By Shoney Marie Ross

Today is the day I make a change,
Today is the day I no longer feel ashamed.
Today is the day I raise my head high,
For today I just know I won't have to cry.

Today is the day I go out and preach,
Because I'm seeking to reach all the meek.
Today is the day I give our father Jehovah praise,
Because it was he who inspired me to change.

"Why change now?" some might say,
They fail to realize that WE are all in a race and the kingdom awaits!
So instead of looking behind, today why don't you keep up the pace?

Join our race for a change is to come,
So young man or woman why don't you put down that gun?
Let's make a change today.

February 16, 2016

D elores Virginia Ross Bauman, born September 22, 1937, in New Orleans, Louisiana is the second oldest of seven children, born to Joseph Sr. and Louise Ross and she attended Fisk Elementary School and McDonough #35 Senior High School.

Married early in life to Lionel Bauman and became the mother of nine children and fourteen grandchildren and seven great-grandchildren. I lost the love of my life to kidney failure in 1985.

Some of my work has been published in several different Anthologies. I received the Editor's Choice Award for my poem "The Woman Inside." Also, I was given the opportunity to contribute to Best Poems of 1996 National Library of Poetry. I was privileged to have shared some of my work with my granddaughter's Junior Class of Warren Easton Fundamental High School in New Orleans, Louisiana.

This book of poems is dedicated and shared with those who I have come to love and has made an impact on me and my families' life and for this I am truly grateful and that's a matter of fact.

Forever Love,
Mama Dee

Our Special Guest Poets

I would also like to give a very special thank you to Michelle Lee Ross, Shoney Marie Ross, and Nnamdi Jude Odelugo for contributing their respective poems. I look forward to reading more poetry from them in the future. All I ask of them is that they keep writing and being creative.

www.ingramcontent.com/pod-product-compliance
Lightning Source LLC
Chambersburg PA
CBHW021444170526
45164CB00001B/378